PRACTICAL JOKER'S HANDBOOK 2

John Dinneen is still living in Cambridge with his wife and son and still playing practical jokes on his friends. They are continuing to get their own back on him. (Unfortunately this occurs increasingly often; many of them having read the first *Practical Joker's Handbook*).

Lucy Maddison is a world-famous illustrator and secret practical joker.

THE PRACTICAL JOKER'S HANDBOOK 2

JOHN DINNEEN

Illustrated by
LUCY MADDISON

MACMILLAN CHILDREN'S BOOKS

First published 1998
by Macmillan Children's Books
a division of Macmillan Publishers Ltd
25 Eccleston Place, London SW1W 9NF
and Basingstoke

Associated companies throughout the world

ISBN 0 330 35524 4

Copyright © John Dinneen 1998
Illustrations copyright © Lucy Maddison 1988

1 3 5 7 9 8 6 4 2

A CIP catalogue record for this book is available from
the British Library.

Printed by Mackays of Chatham plc, Chatham, Kent.

Contents

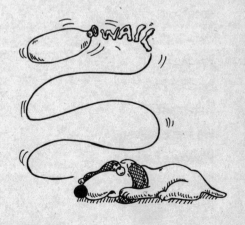

Rules for Practical Jokers

You will have a lot of fun with the practical jokes in this book. They are all harmless but you will be able to bamboozle and befuddle your friends and family with them. There are, however, a few simple rules that practical jokers should always follow:

Choose your victims with care.

Make sure they are someone that will see the funny side of the joke afterwards.

Never play practical jokes on anyone that you think might become upset by it. Upsetting anybody is not a joke, it is just being nasty.

Never try a practical joke that could hurt anyone.

Do not play practical jokes on grown-ups unless you are certain that they will find them funny.

Remember that your victims may well play jokes back on you and then you will have to see the funny side of things!

Lastly, it is a good idea to wear running shoes so you can make a quick getaway!

PUBLISHER'S ANNOUNCEMENT

(Please Read Carefully)

A number of unfortunate incidents have been reported to us due to the last book being printed on Mayog Rocket Paper. Although perfectly safe if kept dry we are pleased to announce that this volume is now being printed on ordinary, less biodegradable paper. However as a large initial batch was printed on Rocket Paper we have devised a simple test which we kindly ask all our readers to carry out:

Moisten the tip of one finger under the tap, shake off excess water then briefly press this finger onto the spot below.

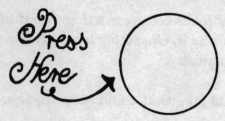

Press Here →

If the spot turns pink or red then your book is printed on ordinary paper and no further action is required.

If there is no colour change then your book is printed on Rocket Paper and we request that you wrap it in a non-transparent plastic bag and take it to your nearest bookshop without delay. They will be pleased to exchange it for one printed on ordinary paper.

THE PUBLISHERS THANK YOU FOR YOUR COOPERATION.

Catch 1

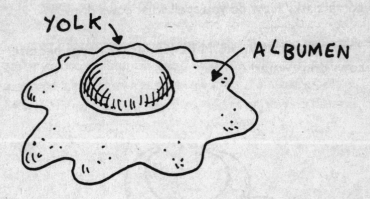

YOLK

ALBUMEN

First ask a friend how they spell JOKE. Next ask them how they spell CHOKE. If they get both of them correct, ask them: "How do you spell the white of an egg?"

Whether they spell it Y-O-K-E or Y-O-L-K, they will be wrong because the white of an egg is the albumen!

Catch 2

Ask a friend to spell MELT and then SILK. If they get them correct ask: "How do you spell what cows drink?"

They will probably spell M-I-L-K which is wrong because cows drink water!

Bug Eyed

Rush up to a friend and quickly
ask: "What's green, got eighteen
legs and two bulging big red eyes?"

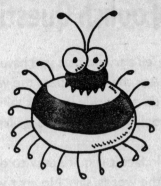

Whatever they answer, you say:
"Well, there's one crawling
up your back ... I'll just squash it
for you!" Which you then pretend
to do very realistically with your hand!

Foolish Question

Tell a friend that you have a difficult challenge for them. Ask them to repeat the words "What am I doing?" thirteen times quickly without taking a breath (you can say that you only managed to do it after a lot of practice).

In fact it is quite easy to do but when they have repeated the words, say: "No, that was only twelve times." They will probably argue a bit but then repeat the words again.

In the same way you should be able to get them to repeat the words a third time. Then, after their last "What am I doing?" you immediately say: "Making a fool of yourself!"

Tricky Challenge

You will find it tricky keeping a straight face when you play this joke on someone.

You will need: a small coin and a cup.

Place the cup on the table under your chin. Wet the coin and press it to your forehead so that it sticks. Raise your eyebrows to wrinkle your forehead and make the coin fall into the cup. Practise this a few times then show a friend how easy it is. Now challenge them to have a go.

You can play a trick on your friend by wetting the coin and pressing it onto their forehead but when you take your hand away, secretly take the coin away as well.

Your friend will think that the coin is still stuck to their forehead and will try very hard to make 'it' fall into the cup – without any success!

Silly Idiot!

Ask a friend to rest the first three fingers of one hand flat on a table, with their little finger and thumb tucked away. Explain that you will ask them three simple questions and that they will have to keep a finger still to answer "Yes" or lift a finger off the table to answer "No".

They must answer the first question using their first finger, the second using their middle finger and the third question using their third finger.

Ask two simple questions such as: "Is your name Sue?" (or whatever), and "Are you wearing brown shoes?"

When they have answered these questions by raising their first and middle fingers or keeping them still ask them a rude or silly question such as: "Are you a silly idiot?"

Your victim will find it impossible to lift their third finger but will have to keep it still instead and so answer "YES!"

Hold It!

You will need: a plastic bowl with a flat bottom, a broom and a stepladder or stool.

Tell your friends that you are going to fill the bowl with water and then make it stick to the ceiling without any support!

Leave the room and pretend to fill the bowl with water. Then holding the empty bowl above your head, carry it carefully back into the room. Climb up the stepladder and press the bowl against the ceiling (you can get an adult to help you do this) and hold it there with the broom. Casually ask one of your friends to hold it for you while you climb down and take the stepladder away.

Your victim will now be stuck holding the broomstick. After they have stewed for a while you can put them out of their misery by knocking the broomstick away!

Slime Ball

Here's how to make your own
Yukky Slimeball.

You will need: 1 cup of flour, 1/4 cup
of salt, a little cooking oil, food colouring,
water and a mixing bowl.

Mix all the ingredients
together, adding enough
water to make a nice
non-sticky, slimy stuff.

You can mould it into horrid
shapes like a giant pet slug, a
snake or a spider.

Make your Slimy Stuff into a ball and
trick someone by asking them to catch
it for you.

Another trick is to hide it in the palm of your hand just
before shaking hands with them!

Hard Boiled

It is amazing how strong eggs are, especially if you hard-boil them. Challenge your friends to see if they can squash a hard-boiled egg in one hand. (It is said to be impossible for even the strongest person to do this.)

Of course, you can play a trick on someone by secretly swapping the hard-boiled egg for an uncooked one!

This trick is best done outdoors!

Sucker!

Secretly make one or two small holes in a drinking straw.
As long as the holes are above the level of your victim's
drink they will not be able to suck anything up!

Handy Andy

Get a friend to put their arms behind their back while you stand behind them and push your arms through theirs. Now pretend that your hands and arms are theirs by scratching their head, rubbing their eyes, blowing their nose, and so on. This can appear surprisingly realistic.

Of course if you go up to a victim and pinch them or tweak their nose you can run off and leave your friend to carry the can!

Edible Spider

Horrify your friends by eating a spider!

To make an edible spider you will need: liquorice strips for the legs, marzipan for the body, black food colouring.

Colour a piece of marzipan with the black food colouring. Mould a piece a bit smaller than a marble into a ball.

Get an adult to carefully cut the liquorice into four thin strips, each about 4 cm long.

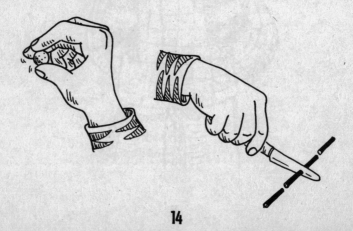

Push the middle of the liquorice legs into the marzipan body so that there are now four legs each side. Mould the body into a spider shape. Allow the marzipan to harden.

Leave your spider in a suitable place. When someone sees it, say: "It's all right, I'll catch it!" Catch it in your hand and pretend it's wriggling and that you do not know what to do with it. Then say: "Oh, I'll just have to pop it into my mouth!" Watch the look of horror on the person's face when you do this . . . and chew it up and swallow it!

. . . and Flies

You can make an edible fly. You will need: coloured marzipan for the bodies and rice paper for the wings.

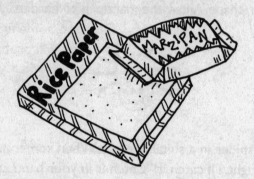

Mould little pellets of marzipan for the bodies.

Cut out little wing shapes from the rice paper and carefully press a pair of these into each body. Allow to set.

Leave a few edible flies on the windowsill. When someone comes in, say: "Oh, look at all these flies!" . . . Pick them up, casually pop them in your mouth, eat them and say: "Yum, they're really lovely!"

FLY-PAPER: Cut out a piece of rice paper 4 cm x 20 cm and stick a few edible flies onto it using flour paste. Now hang it up and it will look like fly-paper. When you have a suitable visitor say: "Oh good, some flies have got stuck." Then you will probably get an interesting reaction when you take the fly-paper down and eat the whole lot, flies and all!

Orange Fangs

Cut some orange peel into two fang shapes. Push one under your top lip and the other under your bottom lip.

Keep your mouth shut until you are ready to give someone a fright!

Twenty-one

Challenge someone to play Twenty-one then drive them mad by winning every time!

You will need: twenty-one coins or other small objects and an opponent.

Put the coins in front of you. Take turns with your opponent to pick up one, two or three coins from the pile. The person that has to pick up the last coin is the loser.

How to win every time:

When your opponent starts, watch how many coins they take each time and always make the number add up to four: for example, if they take 1, you take 3, if they take 2, you take 2, and so on.

If your opponent makes you go first, you must keep count of the coins taken and take either the fourth, eighth, twelfth or sixteenth coin, then continue as before.

The Short Arm

Bet somebody that you can make their arm shorter.

Tell them to stand so that they can just touch a wall with fingers outstretched.

They should now rub the elbow of this arm with the other hand.

Their arm will now appear to be a little shorter!

The person must not move position during the trick.

The Rising Arm

Here is how to make
somebody's arm rise up
on its own.

The person presses their
arm hard against a wall and
counts to 10.

When they move away
from the wall their arm
will rise up on its own!

Missing Fingers

Bet a friend that you can make them lose control of their fingers. Tell them to:

Cross their wrists and put both palms together.

Clasp their hands together tightly with the fingers in between each other.

Now bending the elbows turn their hands downwards, towards the body, then up towards their face.

Now point (without touching) to any of your friend's fingers and say: "Move this finger, move that finger," and so on. If you move quickly from one finger to the next they will find it difficult to move the correct finger.

Gargoyle

Make the ugliest face in the world.

First mess your hair up. Then lift up your eyebrows with your first fingers and pull down the skin under your eyes with your second fingers. Put your third fingers in your nostrils and lift your nose up. Now stick your tongue out!

If you are brave enough you can practise your gargoyle face in front of the mirror.

Now make your face and give someone a scare. Creep up behind them and attract their attention with a horrible noise or look at someone through a window.

Warning: Don't hold this face for too long or you might get stuck with it!

PARTY GAMES

Chimps' Tea Party

Your guests will go ape after this little prank.

You will need: a tape recorder.

At teatime secretly record your guests eating their food.
Later on say that you are going to play them a recording of
the chimps' tea party at the zoo. Watch their faces as they
realize they are listening to themselves.

Mind-Reader

Ask for a volunteer
to try out their
mind-reading powers.

Tell the volunteer to leave the room so that everyone else
can choose an object for them to guess. When they have left
the room tell everyone else the trick: "Everybody is to
pretend that the mind-reader correctly guesses the object of
their second guess every time."

Now call the mind-reader back into the room. Everyone
pretends to concentrate hard on the supposed chosen
object. The first guess may be, say, "The table?" ... everyone
says "No!" Whatever the second guess is, everyone says
"Yes!" and pretends to be surprised at how quickly the mind-
reader guessed it.

Offer them another go ... and the same thing happens ... and
so on. Everyone should pretend to be ever more amazed at
the mind-reader's incredible powers. It can take a long time
before the victim realizes they are being tricked!

Cowpats

Try not to laugh when you watch players tiptoeing over the cowpats . . . even when they are not there!

You will need: 6 plastic plates (or books, etc.) to be the cowpats.

Lay the plates on the floor.

Each player in turn has to carefully look at the cowpats and remember where they are. They are then blindfolded and on the word "Go!" must walk across the room without stepping on a cowpat. Anyone touching a cowpat is out.

You can play a trick on someone by quietly moving some of the cowpats around before saying "Go!"

Another trick is to quietly remove the cowpats altogether and watch the fun!

Ghost Vanish

Put a sheet over yourself and walk about, pretending to be a ghost. Move to an open doorway and, holding the edges of the sheet in your hands, move them up to the door frame as far as you can. You should now be hidden from your audience behind the outstretched sheet.

Move to one side as far as you can while still holding the sheet up, then let the sheet go and quickly dodge to one side.

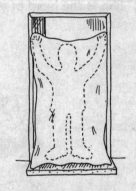

The sheet will fall to the ground and the "ghost" will mysteriously vanish!

Nelson's Eye

You will need an orange for this gruesome stunt.

Ask an adult to cut one end off the orange and then mush the inside up a bit with a knife. Hide the orange in a handkerchief.

First get a helper and ask them to sit in front you. Now choose a victim and either blindfold them or turn the lights down low. Put your victim's hands on your helper's head and say: "This is the head of a very famous person."

Now move your victim's hands to your helper's ears, chin and mouth, saying in turn: "These are his ears ... " etc. Now gently move one of your victim's hands to one of your helper's eyes and say: "This is one of his eyes." Take your victim's other hand, hold one finger and quickly plunge it into the orange, saying: "And this is his other eye!"

The Egyptian Mummy

Here's how to finish off your party with a bang!

You will need: a sheet, a rolled-up newspaper, some towels, and an assistant (who will be the mummy).

Everybody leaves the room except you and the assistant. The assistant lies on the floor.

Make a false head and shoulders with the towels and put them at your assistant's feet. Cover your assistant with the sheet. Remove the assistant's shoes and leave them sticking out near her or his head.

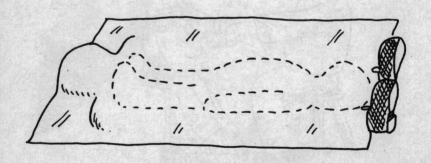

Each person enters the room in turn, bows to what they think is the mummy's head three times and says each time: "O ancient mummy from Egypt, I worship you."

Before they finish the mummy rises up and hits them with the newspaper!

Once players have been hit they can stay to watch others, but they must be sworn to secrecy.

Black Face Soap

You will need: a bar of soap and a small cake of black paint (as used in watercolour paint sets).

Carefully make a hollow in the underside of the soap (you can use a nail file for this). Put the cake of paint in the hollow and carefully mould soap round its edges to fix it in place.

Now anyone using the soap is in for a surprise, for the harder they scrub, the dirtier they get!

Wet Feet

ADULT

CONTAINER

You will need: a plastic container with a screw top – and an adult's help.

Get the adult to make small holes in the bottom of the container with a sharp tool (the sharp end of a pair of scissors will do).

Now if you fill the container with water and screw the lid on tightly the air pressure will stop the water leaking through the holes.

Ask a victim to unscrew the lid for you . . . As soon as they do, the water will leak out through the holes and give them a pair of wet feet!

Embarrassing

Here's how to make someone go red. Ask a victim a few
easy questions such as: "Where do you live?", "Who do you
live with?" and "Who are your friends?"

Then suddenly say: "Tell us who you love the most."

Before they have too long to think, say: "Come on, tell us
who you love the most."

To save them too much embarrassment you can then
explain that all they have to do is, in fact, say: "Who you
love the most."

Round the Bend

Pretend to mishear everything someone says.

For example, if they say: "Shall we go to the park?" you can answer: "Yes it is rather dark."

If they say: "Shall we buy an ice cream?" you can answer: "Yes, I cleaned them yesterday."

In reply to: "How did you get on with your maths?" you can say: "Oh, she's very well thanks." And so on ...

Continue with this and it will not be too long before you drive your victim round the bend.

37

Idiotic No!

Rush up to a friend and quickly say: "Have you heard about the idiot that keeps saying no!"

They will probably say "No?" ... in which case give them a hard stare and say: "Oh, so it's you is it!"

Man-Eating Fish

If your dad is eating fish (say, in the kitchen) . . . shout out:

"Help! Come quickly, there's a Man-Eating Fish in the kitchen!"

You could do the same with chicken or lamb.

Bad Arm

Hold one of your arms and groan as though you have hurt it.
When someone asks what's wrong say:

"I've hurt my arm ... I can only lift it this high." Now raise
your "bad" arm to about shoulder height, then say: "Yesterday
I could raise it this high" – and raise your "bad" arm as high
as you can ... See if your victim gets the joke!

Talking Hand

Paint two eyes on your hand and then add red paint or lipstick for the mouth. Put a handkerchief over your hand for the hair.

Move your thumb up and down slightly to make the mouth move.

You can now have a funny conversation with your talking hand.

Tuff Nut

Pretend to bang your head on a table or door. At the same time secretly bang loudly under the table or behind the door with one hand.

This can look very convincing . . . and make everyone think you are a really tough nut!

Egg Spin

After eating a boiled egg amaze everyone by making the shell spin all on its own.

You will need: half an eggshell and a plate (one with an upward curving rim is best).

Moisten the rim of the plate with water and place the egg shell on the rim. Now tell everyone that you are going to use your brainwaves to make the egg spin.

Hold the plate in your hands and the shell will begin to spin all on its own. By secretly tilting the plate very slightly you can make the shell continue to spin even faster.

Chicken!

Buc! Buc!

Surprise your friends by making a realistic chicken noise ... and then laying an egg!

Have a go at making a sharp, high-pitched "Buc! Buc! Buc!" noise by pursing your lips and then letting the air out suddenly. Next make a sort of high-pitched "Bearh!" noise on the end:

"Buc! Buc! Buc! Bearh!"

With practice you will be able to make a very realistic chicken noise.

If you make your realistic chicken noise while at the same time putting your thumbs under your arms and flapping your elbows, you will surprise your friends ... especially when you sit down, then get up to reveal a freshly laid egg! (Of course, you secretly place the egg there beforehand – a hard-boiled or plastic one is best).

Voices

Learn to be a ventriloquist and throw your voice.

Practise talking without moving your mouth (it is a good idea to do this in front of a mirror).

Have your mouth slightly open. For hard sounds such as B, P & M, move your lips as little as possible. Now you can pretend to have a conversation with an imaginary person.

Here is a good idea to try out:

Get hold of a box or other container and pretend you are speaking to someone inside it. When the lid is shut make the voice softer, muffled or echoey .. . when you open the lid make the voice loud and clear.

WHAT WAS THAT? I CAN'T QUITE HEAR

You can play a joke by pretending that someone is stuck behind a grating or locked in a cupboard and shouting for help! Remember that the more realistically you act (worried, anxious to help, etc.) the more real it will seem.

Giant Sneeze!

Divide your friends into three groups and explain that when you give a signal one group is to shout out "Atchoo!", the second "Atchee!" and the third "Atchaa!" all at the same time.

At a suitable moment give the signal ... and the result will be a giant sneeze!

Tearaways

Pretend to have an argument with a friend, then tear your shirts off!

You will need: discarded shirts for you and your friend.

First partially cut each shirt's seams, for example the ones joining the sleeves and collars (get an adult to help you do this). You can also make small slits in the shirt to make tearing easier.

Now you and your friend can put your shirts on. At a suitable moment pretend to start arguing with your friend. Argue more and more, then pretend to get angry. Now tear off part of your friend's shirt, say a pocket. Next they retaliate by tearing a bit of your shirt ... and so on.

You can continue until you have literally torn the shirts off each other's backs!

Look Up

If you and your friends start looking up and pointing at an imaginary object it is surprising how quickly a crowd gathers!

Choose an imaginary object, such as a flying saucer in the sky or someone on a tall building. Look up, point and say things like:

"Look, there it is!"

"What is it?"

"It must be a flying saucer!"

"It's a silver colour."

And so on ...

Very soon your audience will imagine that they are seeing the same thing too!

Eyeball

Shock your friends with this horrid
little joker!

You will need: a ping-pong ball and paint o...
(permanent paint or pens are best).

Carefully paint an eye onto the ping-pong ball. You can look
at your friend's eye and copy it or look at your own eye in
a mirror. Paint red veins on for extra gruesome effect.
Let the paint dry.

You can now give someone a fright
by
leaving it in a suitable place:
under
a lettuce leaf in a bowl
of salad, floating on
somebody's drink,
or in their bath!

You can also perform the
Eye Out trick on page 50 but
now using your own false
eyeball.

...is a horrid stunt using a rubber ball and a handkerchief.

Hide the ball in the handkerchief. Start rubbing your eye with the handkerchief and say:

"Ow! ... Ow! ... My eye really hurts!" Then after a while ... "It's no use, I'll just have to take it out!"

Pretend to take your eyeball out of its socket, shut your eye and hold up the rubber ball, still hidden in the handkerchief ... everyone will think it is your eyeball. You can give it a massage then pretend to put it back, saying: "Ah, that's much better .. . it always does the trick!"

Invisible Pane

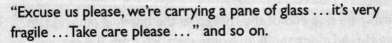

For this trick you will need an assistant and a pair of gloves for both of you.

With your gloves on, both you and your assistant hold your hands up and pretend you are carrying a pane of glass.

Both of you walk carefully, getting people to move out the way by saying things like:

"Excuse us please, we're carrying a pane of glass ... it's very fragile ... Take care please ..." and so on.

Of course you have to keep your hands in roughly the same position all the time.

After a while you and your assistant can stop and carefully pretend to put the pane of glass down and then perform a little skit: One of you walks round and pretends to accidentally bump their nose on the glass ... Then let the glass fall over before just catching it in time, and so on ...

Poltergeist

Mystify your friends with this spooky trick.

You will need: some strong, thin thread (fishing line will do), a white cloth or handkerchief, a drawing pin.

Choose a suitable corner of your room and fix the drawing pin to the wall or woodwork there (about 40 cm above the floor).

Firmly tie one end of the thread to the drawing pin and run the thread along the floor some distance from the corner.

When you are ready to show your friends, turn the lights down and tell them, "There are strange forces in this corner of the room ... Things move about ... It's probably a poltergeist ... Look, I'll show you."

Take the cloth, bunch it in the middle and lay it on the floor, on the thread, near the drawing pin. (All the while secretly keep hold of the loose end of the thread.) Now if you jerk the thread without anyone seeing, the cloth will dance up and down as if by some mysterious force!

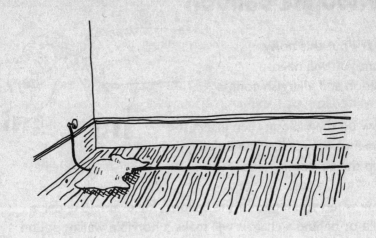

Whoopee Balloon

To try out this noisy stunt you will need: a balloon and a largish coin.

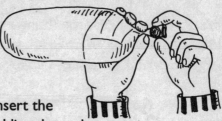

Blow up the balloon then insert the coin into the neck, while holding the end to stop the air coming out.

Now when you let go of the balloon, for example under a table or behind a chair, it will make a horrible wailing sound ... which will continue while you walk away.

Even more scary ... Put your whoopee balloon between a door and its frame, e.g. inside a wardrobe. Then when you carefully shut the door the balloon should stay there blown up. When an unsuspecting victim opens the door the balloon will let off its creepy wail and give them a scare!

SCREECH!

Whoopee Rocket

Make a Whoopee Balloon (using a sausage-shaped balloon is best) but this time, to make it lighter, use a plastic token or large tiddlywink instead of a coin.

Now when you blow up the balloon and let go it will shoot round the room like a rocket . . . emitting its horrible wail!

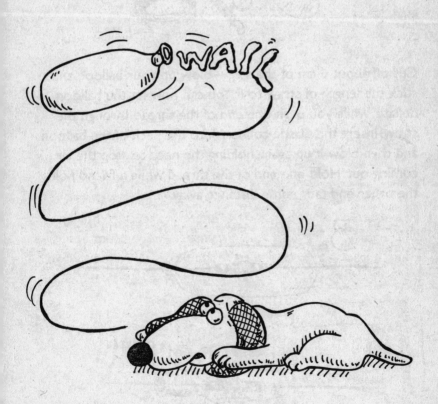

Guided Whoopee

You will need: a balloon (sausage-shaped is best), strong thread, a drinking straw, a plastic counter or tiddlywink and sticky tape.

Cut off about 6 cm of the straw. Blow up your balloon and stick the length of straw to it. You can now let the balloon deflate, while you push one end of the thread through the straw. Insert the plastic counter into the neck of the balloon and then blow it up again, holding the neck to stop the air coming out. Hold one end of the thread while a friend holds the other end taut, some distance away.

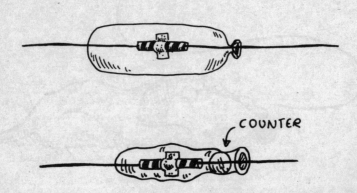

COUNTER

Let the balloon go and it will shoot along the thread to your friend. This can look very funny . . . especially if your friend acts surprised!

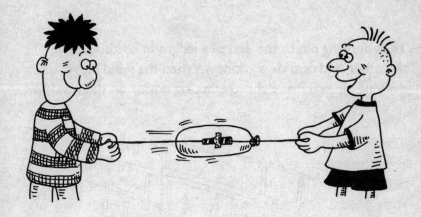

SCARY SOUNDS

Give your friends a fright with these scary sounds ...

Ghostly Tapping

Tie a drawing pin to the end of a length of cotton and fix the other end outside a window. When the wind blows the drawing pin will make ghostly tapping noises on the window.

Horrid Shriek

Scrape a piece of polystyrene against a window and make a horrid shriek!

Eerie Wail

WHOOOOO!

Blow over an empty milk bottle and make an eerie
wailing sound.

Phantom Voices

Make horrid and creepy sounds such as screams, footsteps,
creaking door, growling, etc. Record the sounds on a tape
recorder. Hide the recorder and then play the sounds back
at a suitably spooky moment!

GROWL!

Night Pinger

Here is a traditional way of making a spooky night-time noise.

You will need: some dried peas, a metal tray or large tin and two empty yoghurt pots.

Put one of the yoghurt pots upside down on the tray. Put the other pot on top of it and fill it with dried peas.

Now place the tray and pots in a suitable position, e.g. under someone's bed or on top of a wardrobe.

You can use sticky tape to fix the pots together. Raise the tray off the ground for louder noise.

Just before your victim goes to bed pour some hot water into the top pot. The peas will slowly soak up the water and push themselves out of the cup onto the tray, making loud pinging noises as they do ... giving your victim a night-time scare!

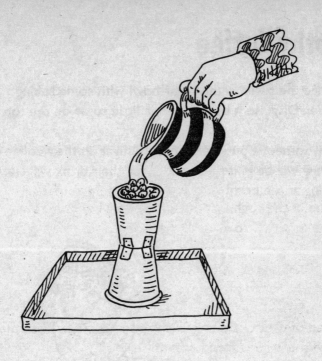

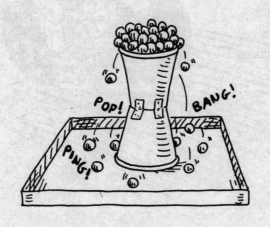

Frothy Coffee

Replace the sugar in the sugar bowl with some baking powder. Disguise it by mixing in a little sugar on the top of it.

When someone puts some of this 'sugar' in their coffee or tea they will be in for a shock … for their drink will start foaming at the brim!

Stick-Down

You will need: a piece of reusable adhesive (e.g. Blu-Tack).

Put a piece of the adhesive (about the size of a large grape) between someone's cup and saucer. Press down gently.

Now when they pick up their cup the saucer will come too!

You can also stick cups and mugs down onto smooth surfaces, but do not do this if they contain hot drinks because the liquid could splash out.

Heavy Weight

Pretend that a large, light object such as a block of polystyrene is extremely heavy. (You can paint it grey or black for extra realism.)

Get a friend to help you, with extreme difficulty, to lift it up and carry it along.

Then give someone a shock by suddenly saying: "Here, catch this!" ... and heaving it at them!

CATCH THIS!

Some People Believe Anything...

A while ago a well-known astronomer invited viewers to take part in a scientific experiment. He told them that Pluto and Jupiter were aligned such that the earth's gravity would be reduced for a few hours ... so if people jumped up in the air they could float! People all over the country began jumping up and down and many phoned in to say that they had indeed floated ... One caller insisted that he had actually hit his head on the ceiling!

Topsy-turvy ...

A number of jokers have gone to the trouble to fix all the
furniture in a room to the ceiling so anyone entering would
think that the world had turned upside down! Wealthy
American prankster Rudolph Shenk had just such a room
with the floor painted white and floorboards painted on the
ceiling. A chandelier stuck up from the middle of the floor.
After his guests had enjoyed a slap-up meal Mr Shenk waited
until they fell fast asleep. He would then wheel one or two
of them into his upside-down room and then observe the
fun in the morning through secret peepholes!

Even Royalty do it ...

If anyone tells you off for playing a practical joke you can
tell them: "Well, the Royal Family plays practical jokes!" It is
well known that the British Royal Family have been very keen
practical jokers. For example, Prince Charles, while a cadet
at RAF college, disguised his voice and announced over the
loudspeaker that there was a fault in the heels of every
cadet's shoes. He asked them to hand them in to the Porter's
Lodge ... and apparently they all fell for it!

And Actors ...

Some years ago during the filming of a Western, the actor Paul Newman and the film's director Robert Altman started playing practical jokes on each other. The joking got out of hand and ended up with the actor's location caravan being completely filled with popcorn! In retaliation Paul Newman put 300 live chickens into Robert Altman's caravan!

Of course your practical jokes do not have to be as elaborate as these. You can have fun with the easy-to-do practical jokes described in this book ... and we wish you the best of luck with them!